**Copyright ©
RND**

All rights reserved. No part of this publication may be reproduced, distributed, or transmitted in any form or by any means, including photocopying, recording, or other electronic or mechanical methods, without the prior written permission of the publisher, except in the case of brief quotations embodied in critical reviews and certain other noncommercial uses permitted by copyright law.

Contents

Introduction 4
    Growth and propagation 7
    Phytochemical study 7
    How to Grow a Costus Igneus Plant 11
        Things Needed 13
        Tips 14
Diabetes 18
    The History of Diabetes 19
    A Modern Epidemic with an Ancient Solution 21
    Insulin and Glucose 23
    Glucagon and Glycogen 27
    Insulin Resistance 31
        For a couple of reasons 35
The Insulin Plant 38
    What does the plant contain 38
    How do I get this plant 39
    Is it safe for human consumption 39
    Is it effective in reducing blood sugar 40
    Does it have any other uses 40
    What does the current research mean 41
    Benefits of Insulin Plant 56
    Insulin Plant Leaves – Miracle Treatment For Diabetes 57

Benefits of Insulin plant in the natural treatment of diabetes 59

Care instructions for insulin plant 60

How to use insulin plant for curing diabetes......................... 62

Conclusion 63

Introduction

Costus igeus, commonly known as insulin plant, belongs to family Costaceae. It is believed that consumption of the leaves helps lower the blood glucose levels, and diabetics who consumed the leaves of this plant report a fall in their blood glucose levels.

Insulin plant, Step ladder, and Spiral flag are a few of the names that have been given to Costus Igneus Nak, also known by its botanical name as Chamaecostus cuspidatus. A plant native to South and Central America, Costus igneus Nak comes from the plant family Costaceae and is among the genus Costus. Consisting of nearly 150 species, Costus is the largest in the family, and found primarily in tropical climates. Though native to the Americas, this plant can be found growing densely in the gardens of Southern India, where has received the nickname "Insulin Plant."

Taxonomy

- Botanical name: Costus igneus N.E.Br
- Domain: Eukaryota
- Kingdom: Plantae
- Subkingdom: Viridaeplantae
- Phylum: Tracheophyta
- Subphylum: Euphyllophytina
- Infraphylum: Radiatopses
- Class: Liliopsida
- Subclass: Commelinidae
- Superorder: Zingiberanae
- Order: Zingiberales
- Family: Costaceae
- Subfamily: Asteroideae
- Tribe: Coreopsideae
- Genus: Costus
- Specific epithet: Igneus

It is a perennial, upright, spreading plant reaching about two feet tall, with the tallest stems falling over and lying on the ground. Leaves are simple, alternate, entire, oblong, evergreen, 4-8 inches in length with parallel venation. The large, smooth, dark green leaves of this tropical evergreen have light purple undersides and are spirally arranged around stems, forming attractive, arching clumps arising from underground rootstocks. Beautiful, 1.5-inch diameter, orange flowers are produced in the warm months, appearing on cone-like heads at the tips of branches.[8] Fruits are inconspicuous, not showy, less than 0.5 inch, and green-colored.

Growth and propagation

Spiral flag grows in either full sun or partial shade. It needs fertile soil and ample moisture, and is often planted near water. Propagation is by division of the clumps, cuttings, or by separating the offsets or plantlets that form below the flower heads. Mites and nematodes can be a problem, especially on light, sandy soil. The plant has no diseases are of major concern.

Phytochemical study

Sequential screening for phytochemicals of C. igneus leaves revealed that it is rich in protein, iron, and antioxidant components such as ascorbic acid, α-tocopherol, β-carotene, terpinoids, steroids, and flavonoids. It was revealed in another study that methanolic extract was found to contain the highest number of phytochemicals such as carbohydrates, triterpenoids, proteins, alkaloids, tannins, saponins, and flavonoids. Preliminary phytochemical evaluation of Insulin plant (C. pictus) revealed that the leaves contain

21.2% fibers. Successive extracts gave 5.2% extractives in petroleum ether, 1.06% in cyclohexane, 1.33% in acetone, and 2.95% in ethanol. Analysis of successive extracts showed presence of steroids in all extracts. The ethanol extract contained alkaloid also. The major component of the ether fraction was bis (2'-ethylhexyl)-1,2-benzenedicarboxylate (59.04%) apart from α-tocopherol and a steroid, ergastanol. Stem showed the presence of a terpenoid compound lupeol and a steroid compound stigmasterol. Bioactive compounds quercetin and diosgenin, a steroidal sapogenin, were isolated from C. igneus rhizome. Trace elemental analysis showed that the leaves and rhizomes of C. pictus contains appreciable amounts of the elements K, Ca, Cr, Mn, Cu, and Zn. Steam distillation of stems, leaves, and rhizomes of C. pictus D. Don yielded clear and yellowish essential oils.

There have been a collection of studies published explaining the positive correlations between the leaves of C. igneus and individuals with diabetes. The leaves are rich in protein, iron and a number of antioxidant components such as B-carotene and a-tocopherol. These properties, in combination with its "natural insulin" content (phyto-compounds that simulate the metabolic action of insulin when ingested), aids in C. igneus' ability to lower blood sugar in individuals with diabetes.

With a healthy stalk standing straight and strong, C. igneus has been given the names, Spiral flag and Step ladder, due to the arrangement of its leaves as they stem from the main stalk in an upwords spiralling manner. Standing between 2-3 feet from the ground, this plant has wide green (ranging from very dark to almost lime colored) leaves that step and spiral up the reddish brown stalk. Among the leaves, which are between 4-8 inches long, one can find vibrant orangish-red flowers that are themselves said to be sweet and nutritious.

Though the primary interest surrounding this plant involves the treatment and management of those suffering with type 1 and type 2 diabetes, there have also been studies focused on the antibacterial, antifungal, and antioxidant properties of the insulin plant as well. With the promise shown in these recent studies, and a truly daunting epidemic of diabetes on our plates, C. igneus appears to be of great benefit to our world.

How to Grow a Costus Igneus Plant

1. Choose a location in either partial sun or partial shade. Plant in partial sun in mild climates and partial shade in hot areas. Costus igneus is a plant that loves water in both soil and air. It is often planted near water. Costus are best planted in the early spring.

2. Dig the holes so that the plants may be set on 2 to 3 foot centers to allow room for growth. Costus do not require deep planting. Dig the bed only 2 or 3 inches deep. You can use Costus igneus in shrub borders to add interest and color to other plantings.

3. Add an organic amendment such as compost or peat moss to the soil to improve drainage. Though they can tolerate acidic, alkaline, clay, sand or loamy soils, Costus grow best in rich,

well-draining soil. Set the Costus igneus rhizomes into position and replace soil. Costus rhizomes are rounded with the scars of the old canes visible. They may still have canes attached. Plant the rhizome about 1 inch deep with the old canes facing upward. Do not plant too deep, which can cause rotting of the rhizome. Cover the rhizome with soil and tamp the soil down firmly with the back of a shovel.

4. Fertilize in the spring with a general purpose fertilizer and then monthly during the summer months.

5. Spread organic mulch such as wood chips around the base of the plants to insulate them during the winter months. Ensure that the mulch does not touch the stalks of the plants. Avoid additional watering during cold weather months.

6. Remove mulch, then water and fertilize the underground rhizomes in the spring to prepare the plant for new growth. Costus requires 1 to 2 inches of water weekly, either through rainfall or irrigation.

7. Apply insecticidal soap for outbreaks of aphids or spider mites. Spray the solution on all surfaces of the plant, including the undersides of the leaves.

Things Needed
- Shovel
- Tape measure
- Organic mulch
- General purpose fertilizer
- Insecticidal soap
- Sharp knife

Note: Costus igneus does not have good salt tolerance and will not grow well close to coastal environments.

Tips
- This variety of Costus grows well as a container plant because of its clumping growth habit.
- Remove the mulch when fertilizing plants. Then replace the mulch.
- Divide the rhizomes with a sharp knife to propagate. Plant the smaller rhizomes in a new location and water well.
- The management of diabetes involves primary and secondary prevention strategies. At-risk individuals with obesity, low physical activity and a family history of disease could be advised interventions to prevent the occurrence of the disease.
- Secondary prevention involves patients who have already developed the disease, with the aim of intervention to prevent complications. This

usually involves the use of drugs and therapies for the specific disorder. As diabetes is a disorder which results from changes in the lifestyle, most studies on primary prevention have involvedthe modification of the same.

- A healthy lifestyle with regular exercise/physical activity and the consumption of a fibre rich, low-calorie healthy diet has been the primary intervention. Lifestyle intervention with a combination of regular physical activityand dietary advice showed an impressive reduction in the risk of developing diabetes in all the studies.

Secondary prevention involves the management of diabetes with an aim to prevent complications. Various studies have shown that the tight control of hyperglycaemia reduces micro vascular complications, and macro vascular. Besides this, control of blood pressure, dyslipidaemia and use of anti-thrombotics form the pillars of overall diabetes management. Control of obesity, dyslipidaemia, blood pressure, insulin resistance, dysglycaemia and the pro-thrombotic and pro-inflammatory states results in lower cardiovascular events. There are Insulin dependent Diabetics and Non insulin dependent Diabetics. The majority of non insulin diabetic patients will fail to respond to diet and oral agents and will eventually require insulin therapy to controlhyperglycaemia. There has been a growing need to develop better and more convenient drugs.

There are certain management issues that are unique to India due to its tradition, culture, geography and people at large. Ayurveda, the science of life, originated in India, more than 5000 years ago. It has been traditionally been used as a system of medicine to promote health and well-being and to relieve ailments using a holistic approach. In this country, a proportion of the population follows this system of medicine, either solely or in combination with allopathic medicine. Diabetes management in Ayurveda includes diet, behaviour and herbal modalities. Various herbs have been reported to be having antihyperglycaemic actions.

Some of these like karela, turmeric, spinach and fenugreek seeds among others, can be the part of a healthy diet. Because the complications of DM are related to glycaemic control, normoglycaemia or near normoglycaemia is the desired, but often elusive, goal for most patients. Regardless of the level of hyperglycaemia, improvement in glycaemic control will lower the risk of diabetes complications. Regular consumption of insulin plant leaves has provided statistically significant glycaemic control and has prevented the onset of diabetic complications when consumed in addition to the past treatments for diabetes.

Diabetes

Diabetes is a chronic disease characterized by high levels of glucose (sugar) in the blood. Diabetes occurs when insulin is not produced in sufficient amounts by the beta cells of the pancreas, or the cells of the body are unable to use insulin in the proper way to metabolize glucose (known as insulin resistance, or decreased insulin sensitivity). Over time high blood glucose levels can lead to serious diabetes complications.

Type 1 diabetes is a chronic and presently incurable and unpreventable disease where the pancreas produces none or very little insulin. It is also called insulin-dependent diabetes.

The most prevalent form of diabetes (more than 90%), type 2 diabetes, is highly preventable. Type 2 diabetes is characterized by insulin resistance, decreased insulin production by the pancreas, or a combination of the two.

Diabetes - A Disease that Crosses All Divides

By 2030 more than 500 million people around the world will be living with type 2 diabetes. It is a rising global epidemic that crosses all divides, but is especially pervasive in minority populations in developed countries like the United States, and is most rapidly growing in developing nations throughout the general populace.

The History of Diabetes

Diabetes has been recognized as a medical problem for thousands of years. In Ancient Egypt a condition described by excessive urination, thirst and weight loss was described in hieroglyphics on papyrus; what today we would call type 1 diabetes. Astute physicians at the time prescribed diets of whole grains to limit the symptoms, a revelation modern researchers are finally rediscovering more than 3,000 years later.

The first clinical test of diabetes was devised in Ancient India, where patients exhibiting the common diabetes symptoms described above, had their urine analyzed with the help of ants. If the sugar-loving ants came rushing to the urine, a diagnosis of "madhumeha" was given, which translates to "honey urine." Diabetics have elevated levels of glucose in the urine, as well as the blood, as the renal system (kidneys) works to expel the excess glucose from the body. Now instead of ants we use things like A1C tests to diagnose diabetes.

The distinction between type 1 and type 2 diabetes was first recognized in India and China around 2,000 years ago, and the causal relationship between obesity and type 2 diabetes was also noted since the symptoms of type 2 diabetes occurred almost exclusively in overweight, affluent, adult individuals. Due to the modern world's propensity for eating cheap processed foods and being sedentary, type 2 diabetes is no longer a "disease of affluence" and has now become more prevalent in poorer communities and cultures.

The word "Diabetes" comes from Ancient Greece and means "to pass through," in reference to the associated frequent urination, and the belief of Greek physicians that diabetes was a disease of the kidneys. Furthermore, "mellitus" means "honeyed" in Greek, so the clinical term "diabetes mellitus" describes something similar to the "madhumeha" diagnosis in Ancient India.

A Modern Epidemic with an Ancient Solution

With all of our modern research, medicines and "understanding," it is a wonder to consider that the essence of what diabetes is, has been understood for thousands of years. In regards to preventable type 2 diabetes, obesity has long been known to be a major risk factor for the disease, specifically in highly populated countries where obesity is now exploding in prevalence, India and China, and type 2 diabetes along with it. The Ancient Egyptians knew that blood glucose levels could be managed through modifications in diet, something the modern world is only recently recognizing the importance of in the prevention and integrated management of diabetes. In a globalized world with rising incidence of chronic diseases like type 2 diabetes, stress and environmental destruction, have we really advanced so much?

Insulin and Glucose

The hormone Insulin is a protein produced by the beta cells within the islets of the pancreas. Insulin is the primary regulator of glucose metabolism, which is the conversion of glucose into energy within the body, as well as the storage of excess glucose that the body doesn't readily need.

Glucose enters the bloodstream principally through the consumption of carbohydrates(sugars and starches). When glucose levels are elevated (meaning when blood sugar is raised), a healthily functioning pancreas secretes insulin to metabolize the glucose, and the glucose is absorbed from the bloodstream into liver cells, muscle cells and fat cells for ready use as energy. Insulin also slows the natural production of glucose by the liver, and aids in the storage of excess glucose. This stored glucose becomes glycogen in muscle and liver tissues, and is ready to be turned back into glucose when blood sugar levels get low. In healthy individuals, these metabolic functions enabled by insulin keep blood sugar levels in a balanced range. This regulation is known as glucose homeostasis.

This integral balance between insulin secretion by the pancreas and glucose levels in the blood can be thrown off in several ways. Insulin resistance, for example, occurs when fat, liver and muscle cells do not absorb glucose from the blood due to a decreased ability to respond to the presence of insulin (lower "insulin sensitivity"). If this circumstance of glucose not being absorbed efficiently into cells persists, the pancreas becomes unable to produce enough insulin to maintain glucose homeostasis, resulting in prediabetes and eventually type 2 diabetes if changes in eating habits and lifestyle are not made. Often insulin resistance is brought on by excessive consumption of refined carbohydrates and processed foods with added sugars, which flood the body with glucose so quickly that the cells become overwhelmed. This process is also closely correlated to obesity, where the excess energy is converted into fat through a process called "lipogenesis."

In type 1 diabetes, on the other hand, it is much more common for the beta cells within the pancreas to become damaged or destroyed, and for the pancreas to stop producing sufficient insulin levels for glucose absorption in the body. This leads to consistently high blood glucose levels and general deterioration of the body.

Type 1 diabetes and certain advanced stages of type 2 diabetes are treated by the administration of biosynthetic human insulin, either through injections or an insulin pump. Until the 1980's, insulin administered to treat diabetes was actually synthesized from animals, such as dogs and pigs, with uncomfortable side effects, and before that there was no effective treatment known for diabetes.

Now human insulin is a rapidly growing multi-billion dollar medical treatment, one of the pharmaceutical industries' greatest treasures. For most who need insulin, it must be taken every day, and with every meal, until death. So with the rising incidence around the world of diabetes and its partner-in-crime obesity, and continued trends towards diets based on refined and processed foods and lifestyles that are urban and sedentary, human insulin might end up challenging water, milk and coca cola as the world's most consumed liquid. This is slightly facetious, of course, but it's no joke that a whole range of factors are pushing diabetes into the mainstream; an almost accepted inevitability of the modern world, all while in truth type 2 diabetes is almost entirely preventable.

Glucagon and Glycogen

Glucagon can be pictured as the antithesis of Insulin in the ongoing saga, and now global tragedy, of blood glucose regulation within the human body.

Glucose metabolism within a healthy human body goes like this: when food is consumed (especially carbohydrates) enzymes in the digestive system break down the compounds into sugars, which enter the bloodstream as the simple sugar (monosaccharide) glucose. As glucose builds up in the blood, the pancreas produces the hormone insulin which transports glucose to cells within the body to be used as energy immediately or stored for future use. Liver cells are especially important for storing unused glucose that otherwise would remain in the blood. Within the liver, glucose becomes stored as a complex sugar (polysaccharide) called glycogen.

This process of glucose absorption into cells leads to a drop in glucose within the blood. At a certain point, blood glucose levels are low enough that the pancreas starts producing another hormone, glucagon, whose function is to communicate to the liver cells to release certain amounts of stored sugar, which is done through receptors that convert glycogen back to glucose and release the glucose into the blood. As the stored sugar is released into the blood, blood glucose levels begin to rise, and cells throughout the body are provided with enough glucose to maintain proper function and energy.

So within a healthy human body, the functions of insulin and glucagon are essential and natural in regulating blood glucose levels and maintaining proper muscular and cognitive function.

Glucagon serves an additional function as well, which is to signal the release of stored fats within the liver through a process known as lipolysis. The release of stored fatty acids from the liver to be used by other tissues within the body, such as skeletal tissues, also helps maintain energy and glucose balance within the body. This particular function of glucagon is important for both healthy individuals and those with type 1 and advanced stages of type 2 diabetes.

When someone has type 1 diabetes, insulin is not produced properly by the cells of the pancreas and must be administered externally in order to metabolize glucose.

Type 2 diabetes usually occurs when the cells of the body stop responding properly to insulin, leading glucose to stay within the bloodstream. Individuals with prediabetes begin to exhibit these signs of insulin resistance, which if not addressed with dietary and lifestyle changes such as eating fresh whole foods and exercising, will often lead to type 2 diabetes. For those with advanced stages of type 2 diabetes, the pancreatic cells that produce insulin eventually become exhausted and stop functioning, and insulin must be administered externally in order to metabolize glucose.

Glucagon is also something of a safety-net for those with type 1, type 2 and prediabetes. Since typically glucose remains in the bloodstream of diabetics long after eating, there is rarely reason for glucagon to be produced by the pancreas in order to release stored sugars and raise blood glucose levels. When too much insulin is externally administered, however, glucagon must be produced in order to prevent hypoglycemia, a dangerous condition where blood sugar levels are too low.

Insulin Resistance

Insulin resistance is an increasingly common and very important risk factor for type 2 diabetes. Insulin resistance occurs when the cells of the body, specifically the muscle, liver and fat cells, stop responding properly to insulin. This leads to glucose remaining in the bloodstream instead of being absorbed for energy and storage.

Over time these elevated blood glucose levels often lead to prediabetes, metabolic syndrome and type 2 diabetes. This is the result of the insulin-producing beta cells in the pancreas becoming overwhelmed by the body's need for more insulin, itself a result of the diminished "insulin sensitivity" of the aforementioned muscle, liver and fat cells. Not enough insulin and glucose absorption to maintain glucose homeostasis translates to diabetes, and if not properly managed, serious diabetes complications like cardiovascular disease.

While prediabetes and diabetes can be diagnosed by measuring fasting glucose levels in the blood and the A1C test, insulin resistance has no such accessible test to this point. It can be diagnosed through measuring insulin levels in the blood (a test called the euglycemic clamp), but this is an expensive and rarely available clinical tool. Typically diagnosis of insulin resistance accompanies a diagnosis of prediabetes or metabolic syndrome, which is not ideal since insulin resistance often occurs first, but these conditions are all very closely linked.

The specific mechanisms that cause insulin resistance are still hot topics for research, but people that are overweight and obese are known to have a much higher likelihood of developing insulin resistance. This is possibly due at least in part to "chronic low-grade inflammation." Some recent research is also suggesting that many people with insulin resistance have added difficulty in losing weight, so it is a potentially dangerous two-way street that is important to never go down in the first place.

Smoking, sleeping problems, and stress may also increase risk of insulin resistance, and are themselves major modifiable risk factors for type 2 diabetes. Genetics, pre-existing medical conditions and certain medications may also increase the risk of developing insulin resistance.

People that are inactive put themselves at substantially increased risk of insulin resistance and eventual diabetes. The physiological reason for this is that physical activity leads to the use of stored glucose for energy, requiring cells to absorb more glucose from the blood and maintaining healthy blood glucose levels. Muscle cells also require more energy, so for fit individuals with good muscle-to-fat ratios, glucose is naturally absorbed from the bloodstream at a greater rate than unfit individuals without the need for extra insulin production. Furthermore, research is demonstrating that regular physical activity actually increases the insulin sensitivity of muscle cells, in effect preventing or reversing insulin resistance. Being sedentary, on the other hand, eliminates all of these potential benefits for glucose metabolism and prolonged sitting itself may be an independent risk factor for type 2 diabetes.

Eating diverse and healthful diets of whole and fresh foods also is important in preventing insulin resistance, and reversing the condition before it leads to diabetes. This is best accomplished by eating dark leafy green vegetables, whole grains and many fresh fruits. These foods are typically high in fiber, micronutrients and phytonutrients, and also have low glycemic indices, which means the body slowly digests and absorbs essential nutrients while avoiding spikes in blood glucose levels. Therefore, less of a strain is put on the beta cells of the pancreas to produce enough insulin, and on cells in the body to absorb vast amounts of glucose at one time.

So like with so many topics related to type 2 diabetes, insulin resistance can be avoided, and reversed, through living healthfully and mindfully.

For a couple of reasons
- Research: There are many plants which have potential antidiabetic diabetic activity infact there are at least 111 plants which are known to reduce blood glucose. However the Indian patent laws do not allow patenting plants and more importantly medicines derived from natural products. I have always had trouble understanding the second clause even if you do some fancy chemical extraction and make a useful substance that was essentially hidden underground for millennia, you wouldn't get a patent in India. Consequently the incentive to exploit the "natural remedies" for commercial gain is very limited. Thus, most of these plants/plant based substances may never reach

the market as a tablet. Does that mean we can't study them or learn from them? Not really one can essentially mimic a natural substance, tweak it, call it bioinspiration and pretend that the molecular structure was an epiphany during a coffee break ! Or at least apply for an AYUSH grant to do some research I'm a novice here, but I guess there can't a better time to apply for AYUSH grants than now. Even if we aren't involved in the business of making drugs, if the natural form is safe enough, we can consume them. Even if the effect is modest.

- Clinical: Apart from the research aspect, there is a huge public craze for cost effective natural remedies or drugs derived from plants. The runaway success of products like BGR34 is a testimony to this. Now you might wonder, if this plant stuff is good, it should have a good scientific backing. Indeed there's a good body of research behind this. But let's be frank – research is often locked behind paywalls. Even when it is 'accessible' it isn't truly accessible to those outside the profession – most people are turned off by graphs,tables and statistics. The idea of this post is to simply strip the complexity off the published scientific literature and bring the reader upto speed on this quirky plant.

The Insulin Plant

This plant belongs to the Costaceae family two species are common, the Costus igneus and the Costus pictus. The leaves of this plant are sometimes taken as supplements for reducing blood sugar. Known as the Spiral flag(insulin chedi in Tamil and Malayalam), the plant can grow upto 2 feet and has colorful flowers.

What does the plant contain

It contains triterpenoids such as α and β amyrin, lupeol, stigmatsterol., Diosgenin etc. That's a lot of active principles- but mostly we are yet to understand how these substances interact with one another and whether isolating them is more useful than the natural mixture in which they are found.

How do I get this plant

The insulin plant can be obtained from a nursery or someone who is already using it. Care should be taken to avoid mistaking some other plant for this. For the purposes of research, the identity of the plant needs to be confirmed by the Botanical Survey of India, Coimbatore. They give an authentication certificate with a number and date.

Is it safe for human consumption

Published Toxicity studies in animals show no major toxic effects in the short term (2). Anecdotal human evidence seems to support this. However one should remember that with plants/plant products, there are a lot of variables one must account for – subspecies, soil, part of the plant, extract or whole leaves, growth in shade vs sunlight etc. Since there are no published long term human studies, we are essentially on our own when consuming this. Consequently, those at risk of hypoglycemia (elderly, recurrent hypos, comorbid illness, kidney diseases) and pregnant women should strictly avoid experimenting on themselves.

Is it effective in reducing blood sugar

Much of the published research on this plant is from animal studies. These animal studies generally show a reduction in blood glucose. Homogeneity is hard to obtain in these studies. Only limited human data is available. The absence of data doesn't mean absence of useful effect though.

Does it have any other uses

These days plenty of drugs reduce glucose. It is only natural to expect more !. Plant products tend to have pleiotropic effects and may well have off target effects which we don't want. There are some of the effects of the insulin plant.

- Hypolipidemic effect
- Antioxidant effect
- Diuretic effect
- Anticancer effect
- Reduces TSH (3)

What does the current research mean

Very little is known about the insulin plant especially the human use of it. However, with the public clamor for natural remedies, there may be a future for this plant/its products. Because of its pleiotropic effects, it might have a role in conditions such as prediabetes, subclinical hypothyroidism apart from diabetes.

The plants come from Andes Mountain in Argentina. These leaves have Latin name of Smallanthus Sonchifolius. Far away in Argentina, the leaves often used by the locals as the herbal medicine therapy.

As its name, insulin leaves are very essential to be used as the herbal medicine to cure diabetic. However, it is not diabetic which can be cured by the leaves but more complicated diseases such as hyper tense, liver illness, and uretic acid.

Bogor Agricultural Institute (IPB) has been doing many research related to this insulin. As a result, it is known that insulin leaves has a lot of fructose in a quite high level so that it can be absorbed and filtered by human digestive enzyme in order to normalize the blood sugar. This is the real fact why insulin leaves are so essential and crucial to be consumed by diabetic survivors. Thus, here are health benefits of insulin plant.

1. Curing Diabetic

As its name, insulin leaves are really important and work best to cure diabetic by pressing the high level of blood sugar inside the body. High level of blood sugar is very dangerous since it can create some organs malfunction and prevent the nutrient flowing along the body.

Drinking the insulin leaves boiling water will optimally work to inject the natural insulin essence to reduce the level of blood sugar.

2. Natural Prebiotic to Smooth Digestion

Insulin leaves has a lot of vitamins and complex essence which work as well as e-coli bacteria, the one which smoothen the human digestion system. Insulin leaves has high level of natural fructose to smoothen the colon function system, therefore, by drinking the herbal potion of insulin leaves will make your excretion process be smoother and better each day.

3. Anti-Bacteria

Insulin leaves also has a function as an anti-bacteria compound. When you have much problem related to your kidneys or urination process, try to consume the insulin leaves potion regularly every day. The extract of insulin leaves will kill all the bad bacteria naturally inside the urinate pipe and automatically help you to smoothen the urination process. You still need to consume much water as well.

4. Natural Anti-Oxide

Oxidation is a natural chemical reaction which can produce free radicals. Those radicals trigger some dangerous illnesses such as cancer because the body cells inside your body can be broken. That is why people are competing to get free from such radicals because it is not only dangerous for the body health but also the skin beauty.

By regularly drinking insulin leaves as the tea or coffee substitution, you can get the extra benefits of insulin leaves which struggle and beat the oxidation process inside your cells. Indeed, that's one of the health benefits of insulin plant.

5. Liver Illness Curing

The disease which attacks your liver might come from various reasons, for an instance poison and fat stuck inside the liver. By having much fat or poison from any unhealthy lifestyle and food consuming, your liver will easily be attacked by diseases such as cancer. Routinely drink insulin leaves will help to return the health of the liver by eroding the poison to slowly out of way from the liver.

6. Kidneys Health

It is started from kidneys infection to kidneys stones which can disturb your healthy. Moreover, it can be worse by the kidney malfunction. Once you get suffer from kidney malfunctions, your kidneys can never been back into normal and you have to do blood washing procedure for the rest of your life. Thus, love your kidneys is very crucial, you may consume insulin leaves potion every day to cure the kidneys problem or just prevent the disease to come.

7. Bladder Health

Problems inside the bladder system might be stimulated by many causes. For example, viruses or lack of water consuming every single day which make you get such difficulties in doing urination. Drinking insulin leaves potion every night before going to bed will stimulate the bladder to work well and smooth the urination process so that you will have such a healthy bladder condition.

8. Blood Pressure Reducing

If your blood pressure is quite too high, the result can be so fatal. There are a lot of cases which people dead due to the hyper tense. Hyper tense can make your heart work extra hard and get your brain to have stroke. Therefore, consuming insulin leaves will help your body to reduce the hyper tense or high blood pressure. At least, you can start drinking the insulin leaves potion once in a day as a therapy.

9. Sore Throat Therapy

What's more health benefits of insulin plant? When you get sore throat, the first thing you feel is painful and a bit itchy down there inside. Sore throat caused by the throat inflammation which usually gets along with influenza. The sensation of sore throat is very hurt that you barely hard to swallow, drink, eat, and even talk. You can consume insulin leaves potion in warm water every morning and night before going to sleep to heal the cure.

10. Cancer Prevention

Preventing is always better than curing. By consuming insulin leaves regularly, the result will as good as prevent the cancer cells inside your body. Insulin leaves has much of anti-oxide particles regularly which will struggle the free radicals that poisoning your body. One of the biggest causes of cancer is the free radicals from such unhealthy environment and food.

11. Immunity Rising

Insulin leaves has natural anti-oxide character, of which automatically increase our body immune system. By having such good and well-maintain immunity, your body will always get healthy and fit. You can start from drinking the tea or coffee you often consume every day with the extract of insulin leaves and honey. Regularly drink it day by day will make your immune system increases slightly and protect your body as well to the illness from any viruses and bacteria.

12. Cholesterol Reducing

If you are having much and high cholesterol level inside your body, you can get easily suffered from any dangerous diseases such as heart attack, stroke, and cancer. Cholesterol is the biggest enemy of the body since you don't want to get sick due to the cholesterol stuck along your vein. Therefore, consuming insulin leaves continuously every day will help your body to remove the cholesterol comes from the food you consume which only has less nutrition and much calorie.

How To Grow Insulin Plants At Home To Cure Diabetes

Are you perturbed thinking about the ill effects of diabetes? Well, a menacing health condition for sure, diabetes does cast a ghastly spell on life. Little did you know, but conditions like diabetes, if left untreated, can take a severe toll on various other organs in the body: the kidneys, eyes, gastrointestinal tracts, and the heart, for instance.Diabetes, in the words of a layman, implies that your sugar level has spiked up by leaps and bounds. It is absolutely crucial to nip in the bud and take control of the disorder before it switches a notch up and creates other bigger problems. Now, it may sound like a lot of work, but medication, exercising, and a little control on a diet can work wonders. However, let's get you schooled about an interesting trick that can cut-down the ill effects of diabetes by large thrilled to learn about it?

Well, are you aware of something known as the insulin plant? Surprisingly miraculous, the Costus igneus or the insulin plant benefits work like magic. Yes, you've read it right! You can kiss goodbye to the side-effects of diabetes with a simple, green plant! Too good to be true, right? Let's not beat around the bush and instead spill the beans on how insulin plants actually work.

The Wonder Plant of Insulin

How Does it Work

Costus igneus is well-reckoned for its lush green foliage. Little were you aware, but extensive studies and experiments have proved that the leaves of the plant are brimming with a chemical that cuts-back the menaces of diabetes. Often used as a promising medicinal plant, chemicals in the insulin leaves reduces the spiked sugar levels in the blood. That's not all about the insulin leaf. The fleshy and vibrant green leaves are a storehouse of valuable nutrients. Wondering what nutrients are packed in the plant? Here's the list:

- Protein
- Terpenoids
- Flavonoids
- Antioxidants
- Ascorbic Acid
- Iron
- B Carotene
- Corosolic Acid and others.

The insulin plant for diabetes is a boon by Mother Nature. What's extra? Bedecking your home with this lovely plant is simple. The benevolent herbaceous plant bears bright, orange flowers too. Isn't that a gorgeous touch of nature within your already beautiful home?

Wondering if planting the Spiral Flag or the Insulin plant is a tedious affair? Well, take a breath of relief because growing the herb indoors is a cakewalk. What's even better? Pests rarely infect the plant! There are a few do's and don'ts when it comes to potting a plant of insulin. Let's dig deep:

Best Advised ways to Grow Insulin Plant at Home

1. Check for an Ideal Location

To reap the best foliage and keep your plant flourishing for the longest of time, it is vital to keep a check on where the plant is potted. Stick to a place that enjoys a flush of the sun but has partial shade as well. It might fascinate you to learn the insulin plant is a sucker for moisture in both air and soil. Therefore, planting it near water is not a problem!

2. Should you Dig Deep when Planting the Costus Igneus

Well, you can steer clear from the trouble of potting your plant too deep. A fair room of 2-3 inches of depth is good enough to allow the plant to grow.

3. Amp up the Quality of the Soil in Which the Plant is Grown

There's a reason why the Fiery Costus is reckoned as an easy-maintenance herb. It can adjust to various textures and the quality of the soil. From loamy soil texture to acidic, clay, sand, or alkaline - the plant and endure it all. However, the herb best thrives in soil that is rich and well-drained. To ensure optimum foliage, add compost to the soil and make it better. You can add fertilizers to double the potency of the soil.

4. A Winter Trick

To insulate the Spiral Flag in winter, scatter wood chips, and other forms of organic mulch around the herb. Keep an eye on nitty-gritty things like the mulch should not be in contact with the plant stem. You can refrain from over-watering the plant in the winter months. The plant blossoms best in temperatures ranging from 35 degrees to 45 degrees. Although the plant hankers for moisture, it is crucial to keep a check that the soil is not brimming with water.

Benefits of Insulin Plant

Insulin plant benefits are amazing. The rich green leaves comprise of corosolic acid, among various other enriching nutrients. This component, when ingested, works the magic by enhancing the secretion of insulin from the pancreas. It triggers high or abated glucose levels in the bloodstream and cures the condition. The anti-diabetic effect of the plant is a winner. Pot Costus igneus at home and bid farewell to the unpleasant effects of diabetes.

Consuming insulin plant could the cheapest and the most effective way of treating diabetes and stabilizing the blood sugar.

Diabetes is one of the most common and popular diseases taking thousands of lives every year not only in the Philippines but also in different countries all around the world. Most diabetic patients usually visit hospitals and medical centers for treatment and medications.

Insulin Plant Leaves – Miracle Treatment For Diabetes

Costus igneus, commonly known as insulin plant in India, is an herbaceous plant which belongs to the family Costaceae. The plant is named so because the research has shown that the leaves of this plant contain a chemical which is potent to induce the release from the insulin from the pancreatic cells present in the human body.

The plant is characterized by fleshy looking leaves which are dark green in color. The leaves are large and are arranged spirally on a strong brown color stem. The plant looks attractive with its long fleshy and sturdy leaves forming clumps which are arising from underground rootstocks. The leaves of insulin plant are rich in protein, iron, and antioxidant components such as ascorbic acid, α-tocopherol, β-carotene, terpenoids, steroids, flavonoids and also contain Corsolic acid.

The insulin plant produces orange colored flowers arising in between the spirally arranged leaves during the summer season. The maximum height of this herbaceous plant reaches to about 2 feet. The flowers do not have produced any significant effect on curing diabetes.

Insulin plant has also got various properties which include hypolipidemic, diuretic, antioxidant, anti-microbial, and anti-cancerous.

Benefits of Insulin plant in the natural treatment of diabetes

Diabetes is a condition where the cells become resistant to insulin and due to unavailability of insulin the body doesn't take up the glucose into the cells to provide energy, and hence excess of blood glucose remains in the blood causing diabetes.

The leaves of insulin plant contain mostly of Corosolic Acid which is found to be beneficial in controlling diabetes. The Corosolic acid present in the green leaves induces the insulin production and thus controls hyperglycemia in the blood.

Care instructions for insulin plant

- Propagation of insulin plant – Insulin plant can be propagated both by root and stem cuttings. Ensure that the rhizome contains at least 3-4 leaves, before separating the plant from the mother plant. Try to choose a place with partial sun or partial shade and dig the soil about an inch or two and plant the rhizome. The same condition applies when you are planting with stem cuttings; ensure that the stem cuttings are about 3-4 inches in length.

- Soil conditions – The insulin plant requires well-aerated and well-drained soil. It does not grow well in salty and sandy soil; however, the plant likes compost soil.

- Temperature – The plant likes warm temperatures and love to grow at 35 to 45 degrees of temperature.

- Water– The insulin plant loves moisture and plenty of water, always ensure that the soil is wet, and water the plants more often. Ensure that the soil is not water-logged.

- Sunlight– Protect your insulin plant from direct sunlight. The insulin plant requires partial sunlight to produce healthy leaves. Also, avoid putting your insulin plant in complete shade. If you are planting it indoors ensure that the plant gets enough light.

How to use insulin plant for curing diabetes

The insulin plant is known to cure diabetes with its active constituent called corsolic acid. This constituent, when ingested by a human, can help the pancreatic cells to release insulin and thus treat higher or lower blood glucose levels in the body.

Allopathic doctors prescribe to chew one healthy leaf of insulin plant, a day for a month to experience the anti-diabetic effect of the plant completely. Do not chew more leaves as the excess of corsolic acid can also lead to severe health risks.

You can also shade dry the leaves of the plant and grind it for daily consumption. The daily consumption of the drug should not increase more than 1 tbsp

If you find leaves of insulin plant to be unpalatable. Try to make a decoction of it by boiling one leaf of the plant with a glass of water.

Conclusion

To conclude, the insulin plant is a potential plant therapy for diabetes. However at present we don't know much about its human use and thus must proceed with caution. It opens up several research areas. If found useful in raw form, it may become one of the cheapest ways of treating diabetes.

CPSIA information can be obtained
at www.ICGtesting.com
Printed in the USA
LVHW021048020523
745876LV00011B/417